TBILISI

CITY GUIDE *for* DESIGN LOVERS

The Travel Colours City Guides are for design-loving travellers who like to explore the trendiest places in each city, for travellers who see themselves as trendsetters. Each City Guide features a curated selection of the best places to "sleep, eat, drink, shop and explore", all of which have been personally tried and tested.

Edition ONE

EDITOR IN CHIEF
STEFANIE FRIESE

PHOTOGRAPHY BY
FLAVIA RENZ

WORDS BY
HANNI HEINRICH

TRENDSCOUTS
ANN SVANIDZE, LEVAN BERULAVA

PUBLISHED BY
FRIESE MEDIA GMBH, 2019
1ST EDITION - SEPTEMBER 2019

PRINTED AND BOUND BY
HARTMANNDRUCK & MEDIEN GMBH IN GERMANY ON FSC CERTIFIED UNCOATED PAPER

ISBN   978-3-9821148-2-8

SAY HELLO
GENERAL ENQUIRIES: hello@travelcolours.de
DISTRIBUTION: sales@travelcolours.de

MORE CITY GUIDES AVAILABLE AT
www.travelcolours.guide

This book is the result of a co-operation between Friese Media GmbH and Adjara Group and has been supported by the Georgian National Tourism Administration and the Tbilisi City Hall.

 ADJARA GROUP

WE TAKE CARE

OF YOU AND OF MOTHER EARTH

We work closely with a family-run printing company that has been printing climate-neutral for years together with ClimatePartner. All our books are printed exclusively on FSC-certified paper.

For design-loving and sophisticated travellers there has not been a suitable city guide about Tbilisi. To meet this need, Travel Colours has produced the Tbilisi Edition from the City Guides for Design Lovers series in co-operation with Adjara Group, the leading Georgian company in hospitality, lifestyle development and agropreneurship. The project has been supported by the Georgian National Tourism Administration and the Tbilisi City Hall.

LEVAN BERULAVA
TREND SCOUT, TBILISI

Being involved in the conceptualisation and development of the company's brands and establishments, Levan is one of the key figures behind the success of the Adjara Group's projects, which have placed Georgia on the world map.

ANN SVANIDZE
TREND SCOUT, TBILISI

Ana is an adventurer and restless explorer. She loves to seek out local experiences on her doorstep. As an entrepreneur and digital storyteller, she is responsible for the digital marketing of the Adjara Group.

STEFANIE FRIESE
FOUNDER & EDITOR IN CHIEF

It has to be nice and a bit different. The desire for lifestyle and design is always guaranteed. As the founder of Travel Colours, Stefanie is always in search of the most beautiful places.

FLAVIA RENZ
PHOTOGRAPHER

Being based in Berlin, Flavia loves to keep herself surrounded by all that is beautiful and yummy. You usually find her standing on any furniture available, just to get that picture framed perfectly.

HANNI HEINRICH
EDITOR

As a writer, Hanni is inspired by people, human behaviour and beaches. Her favourite body lotion is sun blocker factor 50. Born in Merseburg, Germany, she is currently based in Cape Town.

LOVE LETTER

Enchanting courtyards, Moorish facades, churches and temples. Gothic motifs merged with Art Nouveau and stylised Medieval Georgian architectural decor. And, Soviet heritage adds yet another aspect of architectural design. Tbilisi is characterised by many styles and it's no wonder: in the Georgian capital, the most diverse cultures crossed – and, over the centuries, the Caucasian metropolis was reinvented again and again. These multicultural influences have shaped Tbilisi. Persians, Arabs, Turks, Mongols and Russians instilled a bit of their culture and, in 1817, a small German community from Swabia also lived in the area. If one were unknowingly exposed to the capital, one probably would not know where on earth one is at all.

Nowadays some call Tbilisi "The Asian Paris", some "The next Berlin". But, there is currently a spirit of departure from the old and a fierce subconscious drive to create new trends, style and culture.

Today, the Georgian capital is also regarded as one of the emerging fashion heartlands. Since 2015, Tbilisi has its own Fashion Week filled with a lot of cool flair. There are many reasons to visit Tbilisi – whether budget or luxury, action or art, cultural or culinary experiences, Tbilisi has it all.

Stefanie Friese

EDITOR IN CHIEF

SLEEP	13
EAT	37
DRINK	125
SHOP	147
EXPLORE	175

SLEEP

ROOMS HOTEL TBILISI	15
STAMBA HOTEL	21
FABRIKA HOSTEL	27
DESIGN APARTMENTS	33

SLEEP   EAT   DRINK   SHOP   EXPLORE

ROOMS HOTEL TBILISI

TBILISI'S FIRST DESIGN HOTEL

Rooms is located inside a reclaimed eight-storey Soviet-era publishing house, which now has a new facade of reimagined wood and black metal trim. The building cleverly incorporates the history into its design elements, resulting in an effortlessly stylish mix of old-world Tbilisi charm, New York-style Art Deco, and the youthful contemporary energy currently turning the Georgian capital into one of Europe's rising cultural hotspots. Rooms is mystical. Dark glass doors open as one enters the lobby, bellhops attend to guests, while the on-site nouveau American restaurant, The Kitchen, concocts a delectable weekly menu using locally sourced ingredients.

---

14 Merab Kostava St, Tbilisi
www.roomshotels.com

SLEEP   EAT   DRINK   SHOP   EXPLORE

STAMBA HOTEL

LUXURY DESIGN HOTEL

Close to the National Opera Theatre and the Kashveti Church is one of Tbilisi's most popular hotels, Stamba. Once a Soviet-era publishing house, the building has been reshaped into a design hotel showcasing the splendour of this 20th-century landmark. It boasts a glass-bottomed rooftop pool, bookshelves showcasing an impressive collection of international literature and botanical-inspired wallpaper by local artist Maya Sumbadze. Stamba is all about the public spaces: Café Stamba melds into a deliciously fragrant coffee bar and chocolaterie. This opens up onto a buzzing outdoor terrace, which looks onto the hotel's gardens, and is also used as a mini amphitheatre and outdoor exhibition area. In 2018, Stamba was named by Time Magazine as one of its World's 100 Greatest Places.

14 Merab Kostava St, Tbilisi
www.stambahotel.com

STAMBA HOTEL

SLEEP EAT DRINK SHOP EXPLORE

FABRIKA HOSTEL

MULTI-FUNCTIONAL CREATIVE SPACE

In an old Soviet sewing factory in the heart of Tbilisi, the trendy Fabrika Hostel brings the historic neighbourhood back to life. The property mixes old with new: on the outside, barely anything has changed, but inside, stylish furniture exudes a modern flair. Fabrika can accommodate 354 guests. A choice can be made between shared rooms, single rooms and apartments. A highlight is the expansive courtyard housing numerous art studios, workshops and small shops. Fabrika opened in July 2016 and quickly made a name for itself; not only as the best hostel in Tbilisi, but also as a creative hub for locals. Rumour has it that Fabrika is one of the coolest places in the city to hang out and meet new people.

8 Egnate Ninoshvili St, Tbilisi
www.fabrikatbilisi.com

FABRIKA HOSTEL

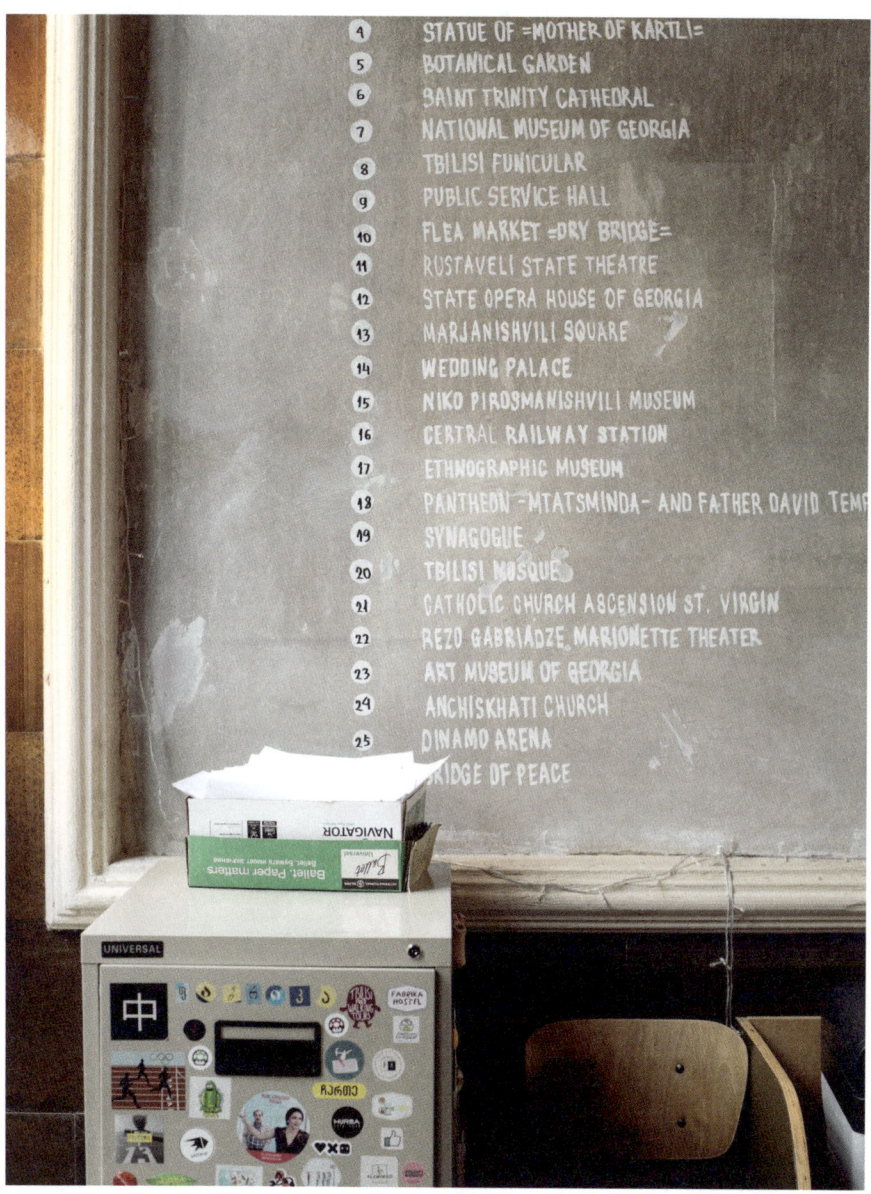

SLEEP   EAT   DRINK   SHOP   EXPLORE

DESIGN APARTMENTS

HOME AWAY FROM HOME

Those who would like to dive into insider knowledge of a local neighbourhood could stay at one of Tbilisi's Design Apartments. Many of them are hidden in narrow streets or tucked away in courtyards, and often housed in curvaceous buildings in the centre of Tbilisi. From the outside, some may seem ramshackle, but once inside, the surprise awaits: all apartments are newly renovated, spacious and bright; yet the memory of the walls still tells stories. The parquet floors and the big windows emphasise elegance and the enchanting old part of Tbilisi. Whether for a weekend retreat or as a long-term rental home, living in a Design Apartment provides a home away from home.

Beyond.roomshotels.com/designapartments

EAT

WITH COFFEE

MILK	39
CHOCOLATERIE & ROASTERY	43
SKOLA COFFEE & WINE BAR	47
COFFEE LAB	51
LILY VANILLY	55
HUMMUS BAR	59
CAFE RAMONA	63
RESTAURANT AT FABRIKA	67
SHIO AT FABRIKA	71
KAKHELEBI	75
SHEMOMECHAMA	79

SLEEP **EAT** DRINK SHOP EXPLORE

MILK

FRESHLY ROASTED COFFEE

Milk is a cosy spot, offering freshly roasted coffee, smoothies, homemade desserts and artisanal ice-cream. But the focus is on the quality of the coffee. Using the famous Italian "La Marzocco" coffee machine, Milk probably makes the best coffee in this neighbourhood. Milk is located in the expansive courtyard of Fabrika Hostel. Its minimalist design blends well with the eclectic vibe and energy of the courtyard. Milkshakes and smoothies can be prepared with a distinctive local touch of Saperavi wine flavour. This is a fine example of a coffee shop that reveals true Georgian flavours and presents a combination of heritage and international specialties.

Egnate Ninoshvili 8, Tbilisi
www.facebook.com/milkatfabrika

MILK

SLEEP **EAT** DRINK SHOP EXPLORE

CHOCOLATERIE & ROASTERY

BEAN-TO-BAR CONCEPT

The bean-to-bar concept is what drives Stamba's boutique Chocolaterie and Roastery. There are at least 10 different flavoured pralines. It is all about healthy, environmentally-friendly, seasonal and natural produce. Coffee and cocoa beans are top quality and ethically sourced directly from South America, Africa and Europe. Homemade smoothies and lemonades are made with natural fruits and vegetables from local farms. Seasonal creations vary from one month to another and guarantee the freshness of ingredients and assortment of Georgian flavours. Health lovers will find options like ginger and spirulina shots and coffee connoisseurs can enjoy in-house roasted coffee. The homemade chocolates and fresh juices will please every type of taste bud.

---

14 Merab Kostava St, Tbilisi
www.stambahotel.com/chocolaterie-roastery

CHOCOLATERIE & ROASTERY

SLEEP **EAT** DRINK SHOP EXPLORE

SKOLA COFFEE & WINE BAR

QUALITY COFFEE & GEORGIAN WINE

Enchanting and experimental. Cultural and culinary. Skola offers quality coffee and Georgian wine on the ground floor of a theatre facing Rustaveli Avenue. Delicacies can be enjoyed in the basement restaurant, alongside the historic Khimerioni space. Their creative community space hosts events and experiential education for adults and children. First opened in 1887, this building underwent significant changes by Soviet architects in the 1980s. Reflecting the local and international outlook of Skola, the cafe was designed by British architectural practice O'Brien Van der Steen using techniques such as gadji (a particular type of local plaster) to create a contemporary yet restrained space within a building that consists of a mix of Baroque, Rococo and Soviet styles.

17 Shota Rustaveli Avenue, Tbilisi
www.skolacoffeewine.business.site

SLEEP **EAT** DRINK SHOP EXPLORE

COFFEE LAB

TRUE TASTE OF COFFEE

Coffee Lab is about more than just drinking coffee. This place is all about creating a coffee experience to remember. Here the palate tastes coffee flavours from fruity to sweet to juicy. Coffee Lab's goal is to change the way people think coffee should taste. Unique aromas are the pride of Coffee Lab. To maintain the coffee's uniqueness and fruitiness, the team sources, roasts and serves some of the most exciting coffee beans from all over the world using traditional and alternative brewing methods. Everyone who is curious about discovering unique tastes is in paradise at Coffee Lab. Apart from coffee, food is also available for breakfast, lunch and dinner.

27 Alexander Kazbegi Ave, Tbilisi
www.coffeelab.ge

COFFEE LAB

SLEEP **EAT** DRINK SHOP EXPLORE

LILY VANILLY

ARTISANAL PASTRIES

Little London in Tbilisi or the "Queen of cakes" is located in Irakli Abashidze Street. Once operating in London, Lily Vanilli opened in Vake serving brunch and snacks daily until 10pm. Single-serve khachapuri, Georgian apple and sour cherry pies alongside some favourites from London, eclairs and pastries, including delicious dairy- and gluten-free options, are also on the menu as well as special orders for events. The bespoke wedding and celebration cake service is available all-year-round, creating beautiful modern cakes for any occasion. Lily Vanilli's interior reminds one of a pastel-coloured vintage milk bar, perfect for meeting friends and discussing the latest fashion.

20 Irakli Abashidze St, Tbilisi
www.facebook.com/lilyvanilli.ge

LILY VANILLY

HUMMUS BAR

MIDDLE EASTERN RESTAURANT

Tbilisi is a hotspot for cultural and culinary currents, which are updated worldwide, such as the veganism and vegetarianism lifestyles. Hummus Bar is a Middle Eastern vegetarian/vegan restaurant with an Israeli inspiration. Everything is made fresh from scratch, on demand. Its motto is "Take a bite from nature" and it creatively takes the vegetarian dining experience to a fresh, new and delicious level. It's tucked away in one of Tbilisi's so-called "Italian backyards", directly across the street from Rustaveli Metro. Here, life flourishes between its wooden facade in a very relaxed way. The quiet, cosy interior makes for a great place to get away from the buzz of the noisy centre.

3 Merab Kostava St, Tbilisi
www.business.facebook.com/hummusbartbilisi

HUMMUS BAR

SLEEP **EAT** DRINK SHOP EXPLORE

CAFE RAMONA

CHARMING NEIGHBOURHOOD CAFÉ

Ramona is situated in Sololaki, once the district of rich merchants and artists. Today, Sololaki equally captivates visitors and locals. Some say that the real, authentic Tbilisi – with its long balconies, hidden yards, faded paintings in the entrance hall, and gilded stair railings – can only be seen here. This neighbourhood café is nestled in a historic building, primarily acting as a home to a famous Georgian writer, after whose character, Ramona, the café took its name. Here one enjoys a great Italian espresso along with mouthwatering fresh cakes, especially the signature homemade carrot cake. Ramona places emphasis on neighbourhood culture. The alluring interior and 19th-century hand-painted ceiling invites visitors to relax and read newspapers over breakfast or lunch.

11 Giga Lortkipanidze St, Tbilisi

SLEEP **EAT** DRINK SHOP EXPLORE

RESTAURANT AT FABRIKA

MIX OF INTERNATIONAL DISHES

Fabrika wouldn't be the popular Fabrika without a restaurant. The farm-to-table restaurant at this hostel features a mix of international dishes. The gastronomic diversity together with a friendly and inviting environment offers a unique social experience for all types of travellers. The restaurant also has a cocktail bar called Cocktails & Dreams. It encapsulates the spirit of Fabrika Hostel with a drinks selection based on local flavours and spices. Vintage armchairs, colourful hammocks and LED neon lights generate a youthful atmosphere full of energy and dynamism.

8 Egnate Ninoshvili St, Tbilisi
www.hostelfabrika.com

SHIO AT FABRIKA

JAPANESE SPECIALITIES

Shio is the first Ramen shop in Georgia and represents another hotspot for culinary trends developed by the Adjara Group. Initially, Shio Ramen opened in the courtyard of Fabrika Hostel. It was so hugely successful, so the group decided to create another one at Café Stamba. Hungry travellers are in heaven at Shio Ramen where the thin noodles are made in-house. It serves Ramen bowls as well as other Japanese specialities and pan-Asian dishes. All ingredients are locally sourced or come straight from Japan. The open kitchen invites Asian cooking inspiration, and the floor-to-ceiling metal shelves emphasise the modern sophistication of Tbilisi.

8 Egnate Ninoshvili St, Tbilisi
www.facebook.com/ShioTbilisi

SLEEP **EAT** DRINK SHOP EXPLORE

KAKHELEBI

HIGH-QUALITY KAKHETIAN CUISINE

Very popular among locals, Kakhelebi is known for its high-quality Kakhetian cuisine. Kakheti is Georgia's premier wine- and meat-producing region. The dishes are mostly of roasted and boiled meat and basic salads – honouring food that nourishes the body after a long day working in the fields. Kakhelebi owner Chichiko Goletiani aims to "increase the potential of Georgian food". Together with local cooks, he has developed an original menu inspired by the kind of food he grew up with in the Kakhetian village of Vachnadziani. Kakhelebi carefully selects the freshest ingredients and prepares them according to the motto: food is conceived from the heart, not from a cookbook.

Kakheti Highway, Tbilisi
www.kakhelebi.ge

KAKHELEBI

SLEEP **EAT** DRINK SHOP EXPLORE

SHEMOMECHAMA

TRUE GEORGIAN KHINKALI

We all have experienced shemomechama, meaning "continuing to eat, even when full". Normally this happens on Christmas Day, but in Georgia, it seems to be common. Georgians know this feeling and this restaurant celebrates it. Offering hearty dishes like khinkali, similar to dumplings with various fillings, this restaurant is known for traditional dishes. Another bestselling dish is mtsvadi, Georgian-style grilled meat skewers. Opening at 11 in the morning, Shemomechama is also popular after a long night out, restoring the body with its warm and rustic food. This legendary place located on Mtskheta Street has brought comfort and homeliness to many.

---

8 Mtskheta St, Tbilisi

www.facebook.com/shemomechama

SHEMOMECHAMA

EAT

WITH WINE

LOLITA	85
THE KITCHEN	89
CAFÈ STAMBA	93
KETO & KOTE	97
ALUBALI	101
CAFE LITERRA	105
KHASHERIA	109
SALOBIE BIA	113
SHAVI LOMI	117
VERIKO	121

SLEEP **EAT** DRINK SHOP EXPLORE

LOLITA

CATERS TO EVERY TASTE

Located across from Rooms Hotel Tbilisi, Lolita serves as the capital's epicentre of contemporary international cuisine. Located in a 19th-century historical building, it is spread over three storeys into a bar, lounge and spaces that could host the most aesthetically dazzling events. The restaurant's menu is inspired by Italian and new American features. Handcrafted cocktails are infused with local ingredients and the urban-style interior including the open kitchen creates a unique social hub. The historic decor reminds one of the various eras in Georgia and provides a cosy atmosphere on the colder days. Guests can sit at the bar for drinks and, later on, bust some moves in the lounge upstairs.

7 Tamar Chovelidze St, Tbilisi
www.roomshotels.com/lolita

SLEEP **EAT** DRINK SHOP EXPLORE

THE KITCHEN

EUROPEAN CUISINE FOR GOURMETS

The Kitchen is one of Tbilisi's most popular restaurants based on the signature farm-to-table concept. Here gourmets dive into European cuisine with special emphasis on French classics. From brunch to lunch and dinner, visitors have a vast choice between Gammon Steak, Lamb Terrine, Salmon Caponata and much more. Vegetarian options are also available and very hungry visitors can always order more sides. The Kitchen remains true to the hotel's signature aesthetics with a combination of traditional and modern design features. Wood and industrial windows contrast with polished glass facades to reflect the city's overall identity. Inside, The Kitchen features white Parisian metro-style tiles and a rough-cut charm.

14 Merab Kostava St, Tbilisi
www.roomshotels.com/the-kitchen

CAFÈ STAMBA

GEORGIAN CULINARY HERITAGE

This former Soviet-era publishing house has been transformed into a design-centric hotel with on-point interiors, a glass-bottomed pool and a grand café.

Cafè Stamba is a true celebration of Georgian culinary heritage. Popular dishes are classics such as chakapuli (lamb stew) and a range of different types of khachapuri (cheese-filled flatbread) straight from the oven. Local flavours embody the company's signature farm-to-table concept through the sourcing of fresh produce and other ingredients from Georgia. The exposed rotisserie and fresh ingredients on display provide a preview of the delicacies visitors can expect. Located on Kostava Street, Cafè Stamba is close to the old town and other attractions like the National Theatre or the Kashveti Church.

---

14 Merab Kostava St, Tbilisi
www.stambahotel.com/cafe-stamba

KETO & KOTE

ONE OF TBILISI'S FINEST RESTAURANTS

Located in the Vera district, this is one of the top restaurants in town, serving Georgian food with an international twist. Owner, chef and artist Ramaz Gemiashvili carefully sources quality ingredients and wines when he is not painting. Popular dishes are the touslet meat with Roquefort and ajika, the Georgian soup-dumpling staple, or the Napoleon-dessert, a Georgian brandy, made with grape residue. Based in a 19th-century building featuring old Georgian balconies and wooden spaces, Keto & Kote also features the owner's paintings. The high ceilinged dining hall and a pretty garden at the top of a winding pathway, unlit by night, provide the perfect scenery for a romantic dinner in the heart of Tbilisi.

3 Mikheil Zandukeli Dead End, Tbilisi
www.facebook.com/ketodakote

ALUBALI

A RETURN TO GEORGIAN ROOTS

Alubali is an artisanal restaurant that offers its guests a return to Georgian roots. Located in a small hidden courtyard behind a metal mesh entrance, this gourmet oasis feels more like a homely botanical patio with various colourful flowers and wooden tables. There is no sign above the entrance, but the name of this backyard is Alubali – "Cherry" in Georgian. Here, guests can enjoy the freshest, lightest and most delectable Georgian food in Tbilisi, with a focus on Megrelian dishes, a region in Western Georgia. The wine list is also carefully curated and offers mostly local products.

6 Ekaladze St, Tbilisi
www.facebook.com/alubali.artisancafe

ALUBALI

SLEEP **EAT** DRINK SHOP EXPLORE

CAFE LITERRA

EXQUISITE CUISINE IN THE GARDEN

Here Georgian cuisine and history meet. Cafe Littera shares a courtyard with the so-called Writers House, built 1903–1905, known for famous philanthropist David Sarajishvili who was also the founder of Georgian brandy production. This house was and still is an important centre of the city's cultural life. Food icon and one of Georgia's top three chefs Tekuna Gachechiladze owns this restaurant where she serves exquisite European cuisine with a touch of modern Georgian dishes. If one wants to experience fusion food and the revolutionary ideas of Gachechiladze, one shouldn't miss visiting Café Littera. Sitting in the garden under the big, old pine tree that is as old as this house itself is a truly pleasurable experience.

13 Machabeli St, Tbilisi
www.facebook.com/cafelittera.cheftekuna

KHASHERIA

GEORGIAN, ANTI-HANGOVER CUISINE

This place is also called Culinarium and is named after the Georgian tripe soup, khashi, which will help to cure hangovers and is designed to nurture human bodies. Initially run like the old gastronomic institution known as the "khashi bar," a 24-hour station for boozers, Khasheria restaurant is an ode to traditional Georgian cooking. Owner and renowned chef Tekuna Gachechiladze is behind this concept, inspired by the curative properties of Georgian sulphur baths and their ability to relieve stress, loosen up sore muscles and, of course, help cure hangovers. Guests can enjoy dishes like the tomato and cucumber salad, Megrelian kharcho and shkmeruli (garlic chicken). The interior is warmly lit and simply furnished.

23 Abano St, Tbilisi
www.facebook.com/culinariumkhasheria.cheftekuna

SALOBIE BIA

HEARTY AND SIMPLE GEORGIAN FOOD

Salobie Bia is a small arty restaurant offering Georgian dishes. It is famous for one meal in particular: the Lobio Kotanshi dish. Lobio is a traditional red beans stew, usually served in a clay pot with cornbread. Apart from hearty and simple Georgian food and generous portions, the restaurant offers carefully selected wines. Located in the Sololaki district, the restaurant is surrounded by historic buildings. The interior design is by owner and chef Giorgi Iosava, who used his personal art collection of modern Georgian artists to decorate the walls. Vintage furniture mixed with memories from the Soviet times and modern objects create a unique atmosphere. Salobie means "a place where people go to eat, especially lobio".

14 Ivane Machabeli St, Tbilisi
www.facebook.com/salobiebia

SALOBIE BIA

SLEEP **EAT** DRINK SHOP EXPLORE

SHAVI LOMI

GEORGIAN FUSION RESTAURANT

Shavi Lomi – one of Georgia's best restaurants – is the brainchild of local celebrity chef Meriko Gubeladze. It serves mainly Georgian food with generous portions and a lot of love from Meriko. Signature dish Gobi (a wooden bowl of Georgian appetisers) is not on the menu, but everyone knows that Shavi Lomi serves it. Popular and always fully booked, Shavi Lomi is located in a private house in one of the oldest areas of Tbilisi. The restaurant also plays homage to Georgia's favourite artist, Niko Pirosmani, a painter whose favourite subjects were animals, a singer named Margarita and feast scenes. A beautiful courtyard full of plants and trees invites one to enjoy carefully selected wines from Georgia.

28 Zurab Kvlividze St, Tbilisi
www.facebook.com/shavilomirestaurant/

SHAVI LOMI

SLEEP **EAT** DRINK SHOP EXPLORE

VERIKO

FINEST GEORGIAN FOOD

Veriko is one of the trendiest restaurants in Tbilisi with a very lively, yet at the same time, laidback casual atmosphere. It offers Georgian traditional dishes with a modern twist and great wines. Vegetarian and vegan options are also available and, of course, the wine list is carefully selected. Located in a former wine factory in the Vera district in the heart of Tbilisi, the spacious restaurant is popular among groups. In summer, the terrace is often fully booked. The interior is inviting with big wooden tables and the lighting, hued in warm orange, stimulates the appetite even further. The secret to its popularity is simple – it's all about warmth and hospitality.

1 Vasil Petriashvili St, Tbilisi
www.facebook.com/verikorestaurant

VERIKO

DRINK

PINK BAR	127
BAUHAUS BAR	131
G.VINO	133
DRAMA BAR	135
POLITIKA	139
AMODI	141
8000 VINTAGES	145

SLEEP   EAT   **DRINK**   SHOP   EXPLORE

PINK BAR

ONE OF THE HOTTEST DRINKING SPOTS

Situated in the city's Vera neighbourhood, known for its bohemian vibes and quaint cafés, the Pink Bar is tucked inside the Stamba Café and caters to every sort of urban adventurer. Relaxed and dynamic during the daytime, perfect for winding down over sophisticated sundowners at night, it is said that the Pink Bar is one of Tbilisi's hottest drinking spots. One can enjoy Georgian wine from nearby vineyards, or sip on a chocolate lagidze – a Georgian traditional lemonade, part of the country's gastronomic heritage. All cocktails are handcrafted and infused with local ingredients. On a summer's evening, it is popular to head out onto the terrace for dessert, or just to soak up the convivial vibe.

---

14 Merab Kostava St, Tbilisi
www.stambahotel.com/pink-bar

PINK BAR

BAUHAUS BAR

OPEN-SPACE BAR AT DEDAENA PARK

The Bauhaus Bar is Tbilisi's trendy bar where people dance on the tables and breakdance on the floor. This open-space bar is the best place to escape the summer heat in the evenings and is extremely popular. On weekends, people stand outside and mingle. Located in Dedaena Park, just five minutes away from Freedom Square, the budget-friendly Bauhaus serves a great variety of cocktails and spirits. Sandwiches, soups, and cheese sticks can be ordered until 2am in the morning, in case one gets hungry while dancing. Occasionally, Bauhaus organises various events such as movie screening, live music, or barbeque days.

Dedaena Park, Tbilisi
www.facebook.com/bauhausbartbilisi

G.VINO

ARTISANAL WINE AND FOOD BAR

g.Vino is an elegant artisanal wine and food bar that has taken the wine experience to new heights. Located in the old district of Tbilisi, Erekle II Street, this modern go-to spot was opened in March 2015. The interior is cosy and glowing with warm light and represents today's contemporary Georgia. At g.Vino one enjoys artisanal cheese boards with a glass of wine or a selection of tapas-style Georgian appetisers as well as most popular traditional dishes with a fresh take. The wine menu focuses on local natural wine producers including some of the best that can be found only in Georgia.

6 Erekle II St, Tbilisi
www.gvinotbilisi.com

DRAMA BAR

POPULAR PRE-CLUBBING VENUE

Located on Rustaveli Avenue in the heart of Tbilisi's Vera district, Drama Bar is a popular pre-party venue before heading to Bassiani, Khidi, or Mtkvari. Dancers pack its outside terrace, dance floor and several different types of bars inside. This bar was once a flat and the layout has been kept, there's even a double bed in one of the party rooms. Local and international DJs play electronic music. Drama Bar shares the building with the Window Project, which presents frequent exhibitions of Georgian contemporary artists and studio works.

37 Shota Rustaveli Ave, Tbilisi
www.facebook.com/dramatbilisi

DRAMA BAR

POLITIKA

VARIETY OF SPIRITS AND COCKTAILS

Politika is both swanky and cool. The modern interior provides a stark contrast to the grey austere exterior of the building. On weekends, its event space hosts live music events. The cocktails are good and the spirits are strong. This colourful bar is pet-friendly, has a special room with an old-fashioned tiled fireplace and cushiony beanbags, ideal for discussing politics, or other things. Politika belongs to the Bauhaus team and hosts a variety of events announced on the bar's Facebook page. Here, one can witness people discussing the environment and youth activism and attending musical events and exhibitions.

164 Aghmashenebeli Ave, Tbilisi
www.facebook.com/politikabybauhaus

SLEEP   EAT   **DRINK**   SHOP   EXPLORE

AMODI

WITH VIEWS OVER THE CITY

To get to this spacious house to enjoy traditional and vegetarian options, or just a good cup of coffee, requires one to climb a hill and some stairs. This is also what amodi means: "come up". Situated on the foothills of the Mtatsminda Mountain (Holy Mountain), the huge veranda overlooks the historical part of Tbilisi. The dishes are dominated by authentic Georgian tastes, with a pinch of European flavours added. The interior is mostly commanded by the Soviet-style of the 1960s with modern details added here and there. Having a drink whilst watching the sunset is very popular at Amodi as the terrace overlooks Tbilisi.

6 Gomi II turn, Tbilisi
www.amodi.business.site

SLEEP   EAT   **DRINK**   SHOP   EXPLORE

8000 VINTAGES

STUPENDOUS SELECTION OF WINE

Tbilisi without a wine shop? Unthinkable. Georgia with its 8000-year history of winemaking attracts numerous wine enthusiasts from different countries. 8000 Vintages has a stupendous selection and the shop is immaculate. Classy and industrial in design, there is a bar at the back for tasting wine. At the front, it also has a number of wines to try both blindfolded and uncovered – 100 new wines every month. An independent testing committee selects the various wine brands during the blind tasting. The shop also offers weekly tasting classes to educate the wine-drinking public of Tbilisi according to the motto: local people are the best connoisseurs of the Georgian wine.

26 Sulkhan Tsintsadze St, Tbilisi
www.8000vintages.ge

SHOP

BUYERS	149
PIERROT LE FOU	153
CERAMIC STUDIO 1300	155
CHAOS CONCEPT STORE	159
CAMORA BASEMENT	163
IERI	165
THEY SAID BOOKS	167
FLYING PAINTER	169
MORE IS LOVE	171

SLEEP   EAT   DRINK   **SHOP**   EXPLORE

BUYERS

CURATED COLLECTIONS OF LUXURY BRANDS

Georgians love fashion and to shop; that is why high-end retailers are paying attention. The former Soviet country is currently experiencing a cultural renaissance, thanks to a new generation of forward-thinking young creatives. Located in a cultural heritage 18th-century building, Buyers is one of those stores that attract many shoppers. From clothing and shoes to handbags, jewellery and beauty, this shop offers curated collections of local and international affordable luxury brands from A to Z, such as By Far, Champion, Veja or Numeroventuno. All products are displayed in a large room, where the smell of the parquet floor adds even more sophisticated romanticism. Carefully selected books and music products are also available at Buyers.

11 Geronti Kikodze St, Tbilisi
www.buyers.ge

PIERROT LE FOU

LUXURY MULTI-BRAND BOUTIQUE

Tbilisi isn't short on style, and with this luxury multibrand store, the city proves this even more. Pierrot le Fou does not represent Georgian brands, but rather all the more international ones such as Jacquemus, Pierre Hardy, Haider Ackermann, Ann Demeulemeester, Maison Margiela, Yohji Yamamoto, Issey Miyake, Rick Owens, Mykita and Linda Farrow.

Named after the 1965 Jean-Luc Godard-directed film (French for "Pierrot the madman"), Pierrot Le Fou also features a fine sprinkling of unique art furnishings from electric-blue Renaissance heads and towering plant vases to circular lighting fixtures and mirrored tables. The store is spacious and provides optimal opportunities to take potential new outfits for a little walk.

31 Abashidze St, Tbilisi

SLEEP   EAT   DRINK   **SHOP**   EXPLORE

CERAMIC STUDIO 1300

HANDCRAFTED & UNIQUE

Why not make an individual souvenir out of ceramics? Or learn pottery? The Ceramic Studio 1300 is a contemporary, artistic and educational space managed by Irine Jibuti and Anastasia Gomelauri since 2015. It is the first contemporary ceramic studio in Georgia and has become renowned for its high-quality production and minimalist style. Located at Fabrika's multifunctional cultural centre in the heart of Tbilisi, the women create handmade colourful ceramics such as mugs, plates, honey and jam spoons, and other pieces of functional artworks including lighting. The studio focuses on the creation of unique, decorative pieces designed for interior and exterior use, including tableware and accessories.

8 Egnate Ninoshvili St, Tbilisi
www.facebook.com/cs1300c

CERAMIC STUDIO 1300

SLEEP   EAT   DRINK   **SHOP**   EXPLORE

CHAOS CONCEPT STORE

OUTSTANDING CHOICE OF PRODUCTS

This is the latest proof of the city's exciting and up-and-coming fashion stronghold. Established in 2016, the store offers women's and men's clothing, footwear, accessories, interior decor and high-tech products. Trendsetters can choose from punk and urban via skater and indie to gothic and classical elegant styles. Chaos Concept Store is definitely the place for the globally-minded, style-conscious youth. The store also displays Georgia's most exciting new designers like Gola Damian or Nicolas Gregorian alongside international brands such as Alexander Wang, Lemaire, Martine Rose or JW Anderson.

14 Merab Kostava St, Tbilisi
www.chaosconceptstore.com

CAMORA BASEMENT

BARBERSHOP FOR MEN ONLY

Most girls in Georgia would die to get an appointment for a haircut at Camora. Some of the country's best hairdressers (and some of the most handsome men) work here. If only Camora wasn't for men. This barbershop offers classic haircuts, hot towel straight razor shaves and a range of professional grooming services for gentlemen. Retro-modern cuts and beard trimming while drinking whiskey is on the schedule here. Girls are welcome to have a cocktail or two at the bar. Located in Fabrika's multifunctional cultural centre, Camora is also a hotspot of like-minded individuals, locals and travellers alike. The barbershop offers a selection of styling products that one can't buy anywhere else in the city.

8 Egnate Ninoshvili St, Tbilisi
www.facebook.com/camorafabrika

SLEEP   EAT   DRINK   **SHOP**   EXPLORE

IERI

GEORGIA-INSPIRED FASHION

This multifunctional concept store sells clothes and accessories by 24 Georgian designers. It is located on the second floor of a historical wine factory in the heart of Tbilisi. "Ieri" means something like look, appearance and attitude. This brand new concept combines a gallery, a coffee spot, a wine bar, a place to meet and, most of all, a place to be. Well-known fashion expert Anka Tsitsishvili is the creative director and the buyer. IERI's aim is to change the stereotypical perception of the country and to develop the fashion retail industry. This is the first store that gathers almost all Georgian brands and Georgia-inspired pieces in one location, that's more accurately described as an "inspiration spot" rather than just a concept store.

1 Vasil Petriashvili St, Tbilisi
www.ieristore.com

SLEEP   EAT   DRINK   **SHOP**   EXPLORE

THEY SAID BOOKS

BOOKS, COFFEE & PRETTY THINGS

Books and coffee is a great concept that works in Tbilisi. Located in the heart of the town and occupying two floors in a green 1930s building, the concept store They Said Books is a culturally empowered space offering coffee and contributes to the progressive approach to contemporary vision and trends. The store focuses on the exploration of lifestyles, culture and design, offering carefully selected books, lifestyle niche magazines and concept brand objects. They Said Books is attempting to neutralise the post-Soviet trauma by trying to act as a cultural activist and introduce a touch of western culture. This store also helps and motivates cities to become encouraging places of culture.

10 Giorgi Akhvlediani St, Tbilisi
www.theysaidbooks.com

SLEEP   EAT   DRINK   **SHOP**   EXPLORE

FLYING PAINTER

WHERE CLOTHES ARE ART OBJECTS

This multibrand concept store is located in Fabrika, Tbilisi's multifunctional creative space. Tbilisi-based artists and creatives such as Eka Ketsbaia, Bobo Mkhitar and Natuka Vatsadze unite here and express themselves through fashion. The collections are more than just beautiful clothing items to wear, they reflect social, political and traditional aspects, for example, the Soviet vintage collection made for Soviet women in the late 1980s, or the Karamaniani collection inspired by heroic Persian epos. The name of the brand – Flying Painter – has its roots in the title of a work by Georgian modernist painter Petre Otskheli, created in 1936 for the film Winged Painter, directed by Leo Esakia.

8 Egnate Ninoshvili St, Tbilisi
www.flyingpainter.com

SLEEP   EAT   DRINK   **SHOP**   EXPLORE

MORE IS LOVE

PARADISE FOR FASHIONISTAS

Tbilisi is now regarded as one of the emerging fashion capitals and each fashion store is more beautiful than the other. One of the most successful is MORE is LOVE, located in a busy, but not the noisiest, part of Tbilisi at 14 Leo Kiacheli Street.

This store is a paradise for fashionistas. It offers impressive and sought-after apparel, accessories and jewellery. The store's founders and fashion buyers Nino Eliava and Ana Mokia focus on talented up-and-coming designers such as Ingorokva and Tatuna as well as famous, but inaccessible brands, like Trademark and Edeline Lee. The interior and furniture are in warm yellow-to-brown colours and were created by Tbilisi-based young architectural studio Objects.

14 Leo Kiacheli St, Tbilisi
www.moreislove.com

EXPLORE

ART AND DESIGN IN TBILISI — 177
MOUNTAIN VIEWS IN KAZBEGI — 207

ART AND DESIGN IN TBILISI

In this explore category you'll find personally selected galleries and art museums to inspire your stay in Tbilisi – a city filled with an eclectic mix of architecture and design.

ROOMS DESIGN	179
GALLERY ARTBEAT	181
WINDOW PROJECT	183
THE NATIONAL GALLERY	185
FOTOGRAFIA	187
ERTI GALLERY	189
LADO GUDIASHVILI EXHIBITION HALL	191
OLD TOWN	193
ABANOTUBANI	197
CHRONICLES OF GEORGIA	199
GARDENIA	201
ART VILLA GARIKULA	205

SLEEP   EAT   DRINK   SHOP   **EXPLORE**

ROOMS DESIGN

INTERIOR AND PRODUCT DESIGN STUDIO

Rooms Design is the brainchild of its founding duo, focusing on hospitality and retail design, residential projects and collectable furniture, lighting and accessories. Founded by Nata Janberidze and Keti Toloraia in 2007, Tbilisi-based Rooms Studio is now represented at widely known galleries such as the Future Perfect Gallery (NYC), Garde (LA), Mint (London), Rossana Orlandi (Milan) and Kolkhoze (Paris) among many others.

Its source of inspiration is traditional Georgian design, going back to the ethnical roots. Rooms represents a dynamic and growing studio exploring and experimenting with new techniques, driven by a love of simplicity, combining the rough with the refined and intuitive forms. The design reflects the duo's attitude, capturing the simple bliss of life.

> 3 D. Toradze Dead End, Tbilisi
> www.rooms.ge/en/

GALLERY ARTBEAT

CONTEMPORARY ART GALLERY

Gallery ArtBeat is a pioneering contemporary art gallery representing mid-career and emerging Georgian artists. The gallery has a significant presence on the international art scene, collaborating with major institutions and museums and taking part in art fairs such as NADA Miami, Untitled Miami, Art Dubai, Artissima and CI. At its permanent Tbilisi location, which opened in 2017 and is housed in a historical building, the gallery hosts both group and solo exhibitions. Visitors can also purchase artist books, prints and art objects at the gallery's gift shop. In addition to its permanent space, ArtBeat runs a Moving Gallery – a pop-up space designed to be moved around different locations to introduce contemporary art where museums and art galleries don't function.

4 Pavle Ingorokva St, Tbilisi
www.projectartbeat.com

SLEEP   EAT   DRINK   SHOP   **EXPLORE**

WINDOW PROJECT

LOCAL AND INTERNATIONAL ARTISTS

The Window Project presents frequent exhibitions of Georgian contemporary artists and studio works as well as international artists and industrial designers. The gallery mainly focuses on promoting young Georgian artists, as well as showing works of a "forgotten" older generation to contribute to the dialogue between the past and the present. Established in 2013, the Window Project merges the concept of public art with a conventional gallery exhibition. Local and international artists are presented in the windows on Tbilisi's central avenue, attracting new audiences for contemporary art. The Window (gallery in vitrine) is located on Rustaveli Avenue and shares the same building as the Drama Bar, close to the Stamba Hotel and the Tbilisi concert hall.

9 Tatishvili St, Tbilisi
www.windowproject.ge

SLEEP   EAT   DRINK   SHOP   **EXPLORE**

THE NATIONAL GALLERY

FINE ART MASTERPIECES

The National Gallery was established in 1920 and is part of the Georgian National Museum (GNM) – a union of different Georgian museums and the largest museum complex in the country – which perpetuates the longstanding museum tradition in Georgia. The gallery building was originally allocated as a Russian military and historic museum, known as the Temple of Glory, intended to showcase the power of the Russian Empire in its colonies. Today, Georgia's National Gallery showcases Georgian fine art masterpieces of the 20th century and temporary exhibitions.

Through the exhibitions, collections and various programmes, the museum network provides educational resources and scientific platforms in Georgia. GNM represents a multifunctional, absolutely audience-oriented space, whose door is always open.

11 Shota Rustaveli Ave, Tbilisi
www.museum.ge

SLEEP   EAT   DRINK   SHOP   **EXPLORE**

FOTOGRAFIA

INSPIRING PHOTOGRAPHY FROM TBILISI

Nestled in the heart of the city on Tabukashvili Street right behind Rustaveli Avenue and the Opera Theatre, is the Fotografia Limited Edition Prints Gallery. A cosy, bright gallery featuring photographs by the most impressive Georgian photographers, spanning the past 40 years of the art within the country. The severe, impressive imagery from the Soviet past intermixes with the conceptual, vivid photography of the 21st century, allowing young and senior photographers to be viewed and appreciated together. The limited edition prints can be enjoyed together with artisanal coffee, local beer or wine from the gallery's coffee shop, the Minimalist. Fotografia also features a collection of books, postcards and unlimited edition prints.

21/4 Revaz Tabukashvili St, Tbilisi
www.fotografia.ge

SLEEP   EAT   DRINK   SHOP   **EXPLORE**

ERTI GALLERY

PROMOTING GEORGIAN CONTEMPORARY ART

Erti Gallery focuses on contemporary art in Georgia and abroad to create various opportunities for Georgian artists' self-expression in the international sphere. Often the art pieces have a strong visual and cognitive impact. The exhibition programme contains painting, photography, and a distinctive combination of new media art, video and installation-based work and drawing. A big priority at the Erti Gallery is discovering, promoting and building long-lasting relationships and collaboration between artists, collectors and cultural institutions as the gallery works closely with established and emerging Georgian artists. The gallery is located close to Tbilisi's old town and is only a few walking minutes away from the Project ArtBeat.

---

19 Ingorokva St / 5 9 April St, Tbilisi
www.ertigallery.com

SLEEP   EAT   DRINK   SHOP   **EXPLORE**

LADO GUDIASHVILI EXHIBITION HALL

DEDICATED TO THE PAINTER AND ARTIST

The Lado Gudiashvili Foundation is an exhibition hall dedicated to versatile painter and artist Lado Gudiashvili. The gallery and exhibition hall, founded in 2011, is currently one of Georgia's most outstanding exhibition spaces. Created by personalities, distinguished by their artistic merits as well as by their individual charm, and their captivating artistic perception of the world, the exhibition hall comprises various exhibition spaces, which, together with Gudiashvili's permanent exhibition, offers visitors the possibility of viewing exhibitions by contemporary artists and of familiarising themselves with various programmes and events. The artwork changes regularly and visitors can acquaint themselves with creative works from Gudiashvili's various periods.

11 Lado Gudiashvili St, Tbilisi
www.ladogudiashvili.ge

SLEEP   EAT   DRINK   SHOP   **EXPLORE**

OLD TOWN

ENCHANTING AND PICTURESQUE

Tbilisi's Old Town is a labyrinth of narrow, tight and winding streets where wooden balconies overlook the space. Mysterious doorways lead to hidden courtyards and often into stunning and stylish concept stores. Here and there one sees ancient vines climbing up towards the sky, using anything vertical for support. Parts of Tbilisi's Old Town have been extensively renovated, though far more of these twisting alleys remain untouched. Although cracked and crumbling, the Old Town is delightful, enchanting, picturesque and real, interwoven with European, classical Russian and Art Nouveau architecture. "The fabulous land" is how Alexander Pushkin described Tbilisi, Georgia's capital since the fifth century.

Old City, Tbilisi

ABANOTUBANI

THE SULPHUR BATH DISTRICT OF TBILISI

Sitting on sulphuric water and thermal springs, Tbilisi is known for its thermal baths to which people have flocked for 2 000 years. The hot sulphuric waters have long been fabled to possess magical healing qualities. Even the Persian king, Agha Mohammad Khan, soaked there in 1795 as part of an antiageing procedure. When he found his condition remained unchanged, he razed Tbilisi to the ground. The bath district of Tbilisi that holds the sulphuric water is called Abanotubani. Visitors know when they are nearby as the smell of foul egg is prominent. Public baths are split into male and female and the private baths, aimed at tourists, are more highly priced.

Abano St, Tbilisi

SLEEP   EAT   DRINK   SHOP   **EXPLORE**

CHRONICLES OF GEORGIA

SPECTACULAR MONUMENT IN TBILISI

This monument, also known as the Stonehenge of Tbilisi, is located near the Tbilisi Sea. Chronicles of Georgia is made of columns, set on a hill. It chronicles Georgia's history. There are 16 pillars that are between 30–35 metres tall. The top part of the statue features the kings and queens of Georgia, the lower part portrays the life of Christ. A grapevine cross of St. Nino and a chapel can be visited there as well. The dark sculpture can be seen from the highway if one pays attention. Created by Georgian-born and Soviet-trained sculptor Zurab Tsereteli, the creation of the Chronicles began in 1985, but was never finished.

Chronicles of Georgia Temqa, Tbilisi

GARDENIA

BEAUTIFUL GARDEN OASIS

This is where Tbilisi's fairies live: Gardenia Shevardnadze. Perched on top of a hill, this garden and tea house is perfect for lazy Sundays and atmospheric evenings. The owner, Zura Shevardnadze, learned gardening in Germany and upon his return to Georgia, he decided to open "a garden for everyone." Visitors can come and buy plants or spend time admiring the natural beauty of the gardens over an array of cakes, juices, coffees and teas. The café also has great lunch and dinner options with a selection of traditional Georgian dishes. Gardenia also offers "green lessons" in gardening for children, and provides landscape architecture and event decoration services.

Nikoloz Khudadovi St, Tbilisi
www.gardenia.ge

GARDENIA

SLEEP   EAT   DRINK   SHOP   **EXPLORE**

ART VILLA GARIKULA

WHERE ARTISTS COME TOGETHER

Art Villa Garikula is a place where artists from all over the world come together to exchange ideas and implement different projects. Together with other private art institutions, the art villa filled the vacuum resulting from the Soviet Union's breakdown and became a significant player in the reorganisation of cultural life in post-Soviet Georgia. Today, Garikula is a successful example, developing creative and innovative projects based on experiential learning, artist-in-residence programmes, or the annual international festival of contemporary art, Fest i Nova, in honour of the Zdanevich brothers, well-known artists in Georgia. Located on a wine farm only one hour's drive from Tbilisi, Art Villa Garikula also produces sparkling wine.

Garikula Village, Georgia
www.garikula.com

MOUNTAIN VIEWS IN KAZBEGI

Kazbegi is a small town located in a beautiful valley surrounded by the Kazbek Mountain. The highest peak in the country at 5 047 metres, it is only 10km away from the Russian border. Mount Kazbek has been an inspiration for poets and writers, steeped in Greek myths and Georgian legends. Climbing its peak is sure to be an unforgettable experience. And for those who prefer to relax in one of the most scenic locations in Georgia, we have covered Rooms Hotel Kazbegi.

ROOMS HOTEL KAZBEGI   211

SLEEP   EAT   DRINK   SHOP   **EXPLORE**

ROOMS HOTEL KAZBEGI

SPECTACULAR MOUNTAIN SCENERY

A one-time Soviet sanatorium, amid spectacular mountain scenery, has had a modern makeover to become the Rooms Hotel Kazbegi. Here East meets West. Flawless service from the bedecked-in-red staff adds to the chic decor, which seems all the more whimsical in the heart of Georgia's lush nature. Offering mountain or forest views, Kazbegi has a large heated indoor pool where swimmers stay warm while gazing at the snow. In summer, there are loungers on the terrace. Guestrooms are similar at this design-centric hotel, yet here and there is a different splash of colour adding more space, and enhancing Instagrammable visual appeal. Rooms Hotel Kazbegi is the sister hotel to Rooms Hotel Tbilisi.

1 V.gorgasali St, Stepantsminda
www.roomshotels.com/kazbegi

8000 VINTAGES	145
ABANOTUBANI	197
ALUBALI	101
AMODI	141
ART AND DESIGN IN TBILISI	177
ART VILLA GARIKULA	205
BAUHAUS BAR	131
BUYERS	149
CAFE LITERRA	105
CAFE RAMONA	63
CAFÈ STAMBA	93
CAMORA BASEMENT	163
CERAMIC STUDIO 1300	155
CHAOS CONCEPT STORE	159
CHOCOLATERIE & ROASTERY	43
CHRONICLES OF GEORGIA	199
COFFEE LAB	51
DESIGN APARTMENTS	33
DRAMA BAR	135
ERTI GALLERY	189
FABRIKA HOSTEL	27
FLYING PAINTER	169
FOTOGRAFIA	187
GALLERY ARTBEAT	181
GARDENIA	201
G.VINO	133
HUMMUS BAR	59
IERI	165
KAKHELEBI	75

KETO & KOTE	97
KHASHERIA	109
LADO GUDIASHVILI EXHIBITION HALL	191
LILY VANILLY	55
LOLITA	85
MILK	39
MORE IS LOVE	171
MOUNTAIN VIEWS IN KAZBEGI	207
OLD TOWN	193
PIERROT LE FOU	153
PINK BAR	127
POLITIKA	139
RESTAURANT AT FABRIKA	67
ROOMS DESIGN	179
ROOMS HOTEL KAZBEGI	211
ROOMS HOTEL TBILISI	15
SALOBIE BIA	113
SHAVI LOMI	117
SHEMOMECHAMA	79
SHIO AT FABRIKA	71
SKOLA COFFEE & WINE BAR	47
STAMBA HOTEL	21
THE KITCHEN	89
THE NATIONAL GALLERY	185
THEY SAID BOOKS	167
VERIKO	121
WINDOW PROJECT	183

COPYRIGHT

© Travel Colours, 2019. All rights reserved. No part of this book may be copied, stored in a retrieval system, or transmitted in any form by any means, electronic, mechanical, recording or otherwise, except brief extracts for the purpose of review, and no part of this book may be sold or hired, without the written permission of the copyright owner.

...

The information in this Travel Colours Guide is checked regularly. Every effort has been made to ensure that this book is up-to-date as possible at the time of going to press. Although the authors have taken all reasonable care in preparing this book, we make no warranty about the accuracy or completeness of its content and, to the maximum extent permitted, disclaim all liability arising from its use.

...

Text Copyright © TravelColours, 2019
Photographs Copyright © TravelColours, 2019
(unless otherwise mentioned)

The publisher would like to thank the following for their kind permission to reproduce their photographs:

Ana Gabashvili p. 6 picture on the top, 16, 92, 208; Erin Wulfsohn (@erinwulfsohn) for Pursch Artistes (@purscharistes) p. 7 picture on the bottom; Freunde von Freunden, Adjara Group p. 210, 212, 213; Nick Paniashvili p. 214.

BERLIN
CAPE TOWN
MILAN
PALMA DE MALLORCA
PARIS
REYKJAVÍK

MORE AVAILABLE AT
www.travelcolours.guide